US MILITARY

US SPACE FORCE

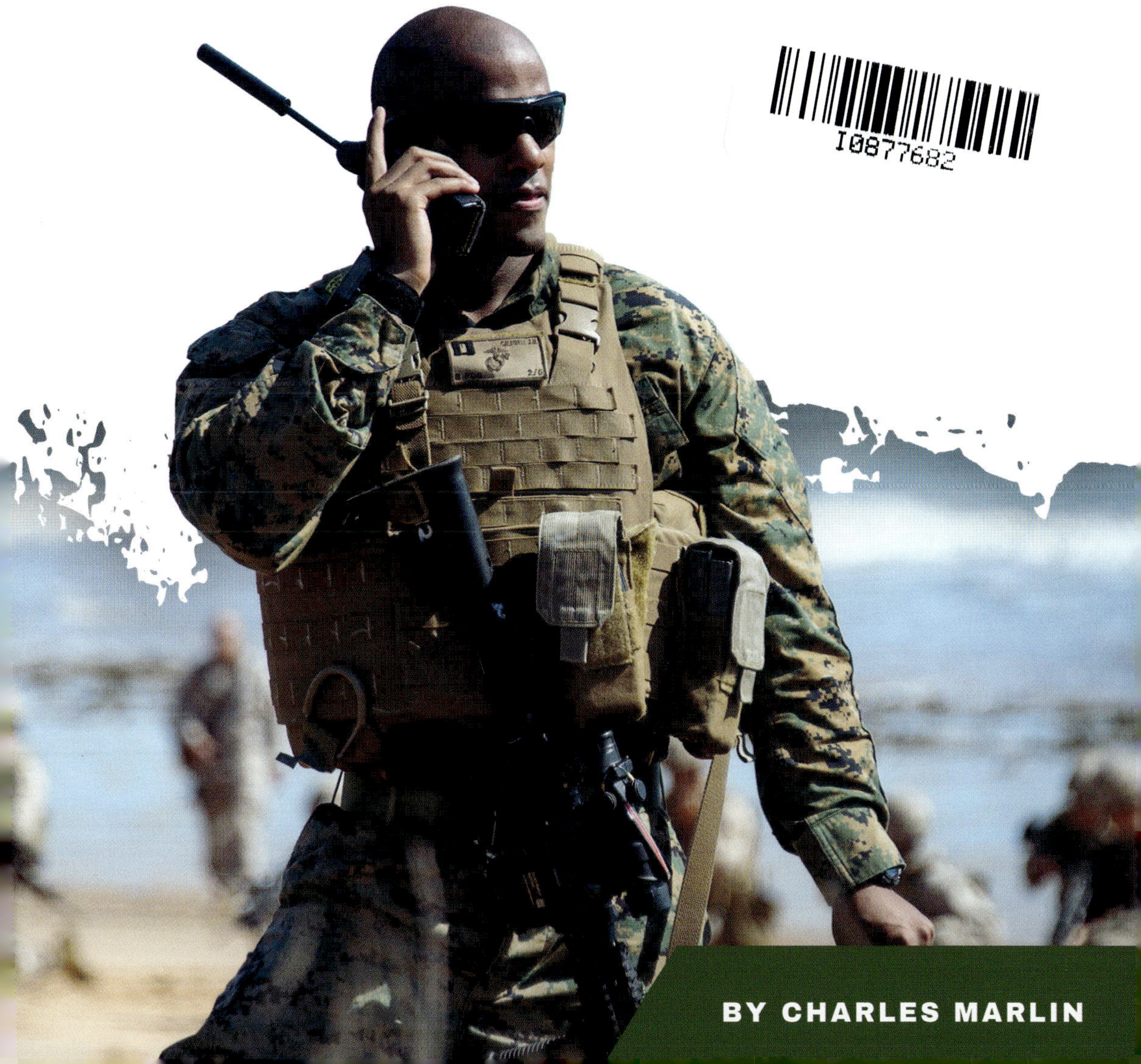

BY CHARLES MARLIN

WWW.APEXEDITIONS.COM

Apex is distributed by North Star Editions:
sales@northstareditions.com | 888-417-0195

Produced for Apex by Red Line Editorial.

Photographs ©: SpaceX, cover; Mass Communication Specialist 2nd Class Daniel M. Young/US Navy/DVIDS, 1, 27; Senior Airman Dakota Raub/US Space Force/DVIDS, 4–5; Alex G. Perez/AGPfoto/Sipa USA/AP Images, 6; James Rainier/US Air Force/DVIDS, 7, 29; Senior Airman Haley N. Blevins/US Space Force/DVIDS, 8–9; Airman 1st Class Thomas Sjoberg/US Space Force/DVIDS, 10–11; Senior Airman Danielle McBride/US Space Force/DVIDS, 12–13; Airman 1st Class Olga Houtsma/US Space Force/DVIDS, 14; Van Ha/DVIDS, 16–17; Ethan Johnson/US Space Force/DVIDS, 18–19; 2nd Lt. Jacob Willoughby/US Space Force/DVIDS, 20; Staff Sgt. Michael Ward/US Air Force/DVIDS, 21; NASA/DVIDS, 22–23; United States Space Force/AP Images, 24–25

Library of Congress Control Number: 2025939211

ISBN
979-8-89250-807-0 (hardcover)
979-8-89250-836-0 (paperback)
979-8-89250-891-9 (ebook pdf)
979-8-89250-865-0 (hosted ebook)

Printed in the United States of America
Mankato, MN
012026

NOTE TO PARENTS AND EDUCATORS

Apex books are designed to build literacy skills in striving readers. Exciting, high-interest content attracts and holds readers' attention. The text is carefully leveled to allow students to achieve success quickly. Additional features, such as bolded glossary words for difficult terms, help build comprehension.

TABLE OF CONTENTS

CHAPTER 1

LIFTING OFF

A rocket's engines roar. Flames and smoke cover a launchpad. The rocket streaks into the air.

A rocket lifts off at Cape Canaveral Space Force Station on August 4, 2022.

Space Force launches often use Atlas V rockets. The rockets fly faster than the speed of sound.

Once the rocket reaches space, a **satellite** separates from it. Down on the ground, US Space Force Guardians get to work. They test the satellite's **sensors**.

WORKING TOGETHER

Several companies help the Space Force with launches. SpaceX is one of them. The companies work to make newer, better rockets. Teaming up also helps launches cost less.

Some parts of rockets are reusable. They can land and launch again.

Soon, the satellite is ready to go. It's now part of a network. Many satellites work together.

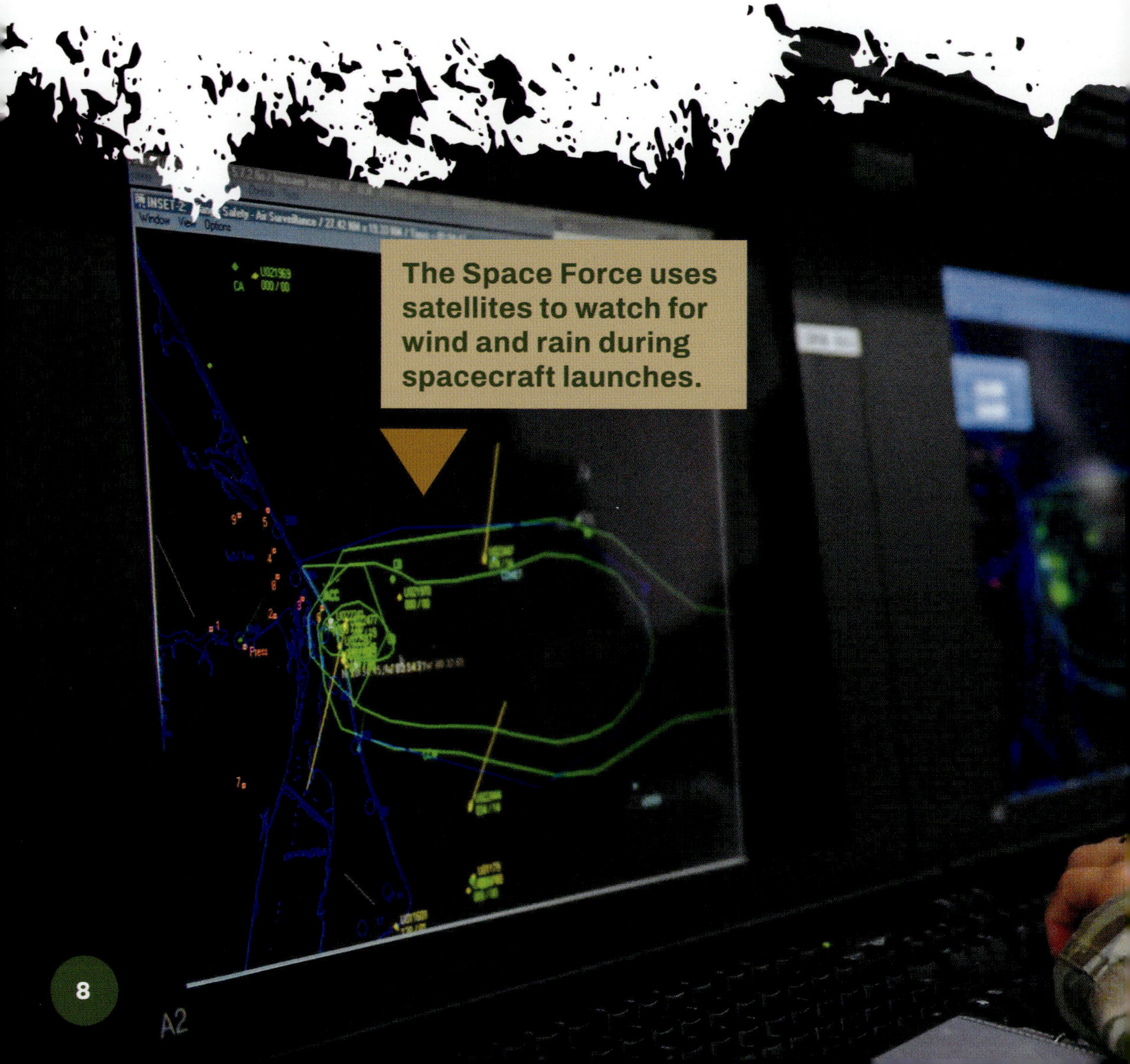

The Space Force uses satellites to watch for wind and rain during spacecraft launches.

They watch out for enemy attacks. They can track **missile** launches around the world.

CHAPTER 2

A NEW BRANCH

The Space Force is the newest branch of the US military. It formed on December 20, 2019.

General John W. Raymond was the first leader of the US Space Force.

The US military has had spacecraft and satellites since the 1950s. Several branches used them. But this work wasn't very organized. US leaders wanted one branch to be in charge. So, they started the Space Force.

TESTING AND TRACKING

The Space Force has six bases. Some bases focus on launches. Some track and control satellites. Others research and test new technology.

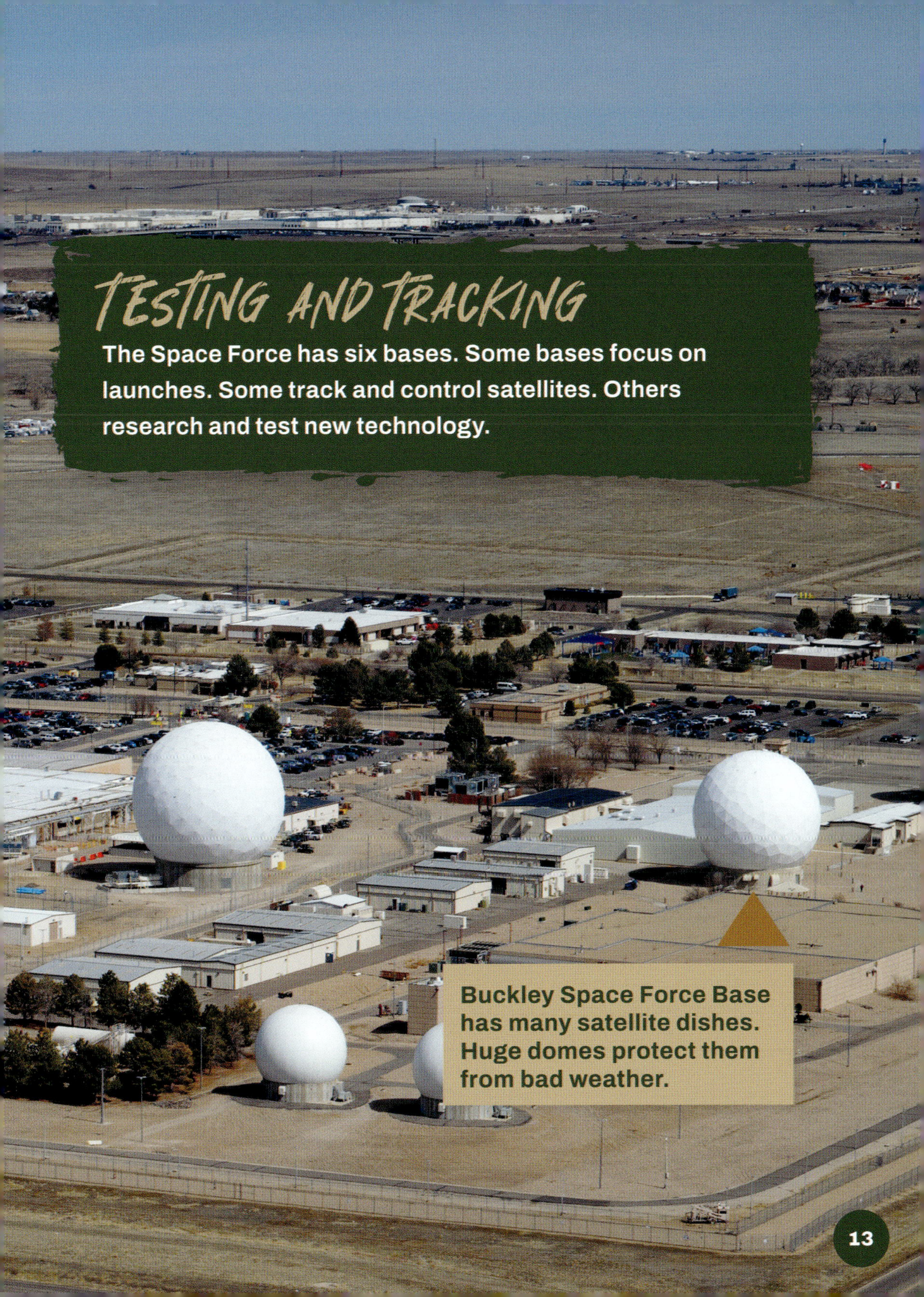

Buckley Space Force Base has many satellite dishes. Huge domes protect them from bad weather.

SPACEX

The Space Force took over some of the other branches' tasks and **equipment**. It began overseeing launches for them. And it improved many machines and tools.

FAST FACT

The Space Force uses a satellite to keep track of all the objects **orbiting** Earth. The Air Force used to do this.

Many launches take place at Vandenberg Space Force Base in California.

CHAPTER 3

DIFFERENT DUTIES

People in the Space Force are called Guardians. They have lots of different jobs. Some require college degrees. **Civilian** workers may do these jobs.

Guardians need college degrees for jobs that use lots of math and science. Engineering is one example.

Other Guardians enlist in the military. They go through basic training. They also take knowledge tests. They get jobs based on their skills.

FAST FACT

During basic training, Guardians take classes about space and Space Force history.

People do tough workouts as part of basic training. They also learn how to deal with stress.

The Space Force and the Air Force often work together to solve problems.

The Space Force also has officers. They lead other people. Some officers manage launches. Others plan spy missions. And some lead teams of scientists.

SPACE COLLEGE

Many officers attend the US Air Force Academy. They complete the school's space program. In it, they learn how to design satellites. They also learn to plan battles in space.

Some Space Force officers teach classes at the Air Force Academy.

CHAPTER 4

IMPORTANT WORK

Much of the Space Force's work involves military satellites. Guardians look out for problems. Space **debris** is one. It can hit and damage satellites.

By 2025, more than 40,000 objects orbited Earth. They sometimes crashed into one another.

Attacks are another threat. Enemies may use **hacks**. They try to harm US satellites or computers. Guardians try to prevent this. They create programs that block hacks.

SECRET SCIENCE

Space Force scientists help make new technology. They also test new aircraft. Most of this work is kept secret. But one known example is the X-37B. It's a robotic space plane.

The X-37B doesn't carry any people. Computers control it.

Space Force satellites send many signals. Some signals are used by phones. Others are part of GPS. GPS helps show people where to go.

FAST FACT

Some of the Space Force's satellites can guide missiles.

Satellites help cell phone towers work. They also send signals directly to satphones (pictured).

COMPREHENSION QUESTIONS

Write your answers on a separate piece of paper.

1. Write a few sentences explaining the main ideas of Chapter 2.
2. What kind of job would you want to do if you were in the Space Force? Why?
3. How many bases does the Space Force have?
   - **A.** 6
   - **B.** 20
   - **C.** 37
4. Why might Space Force scientists keep their work secret?
   - **A.** so that enemies don't know what the Space Force can do
   - **B.** so that the Space Force can't use their work
   - **C.** so that their work will never get done

5. What does **network** mean in this book?

*Soon, the satellite is ready to go. It's now part of a **network**. Many satellites work together.*

A. a type of rocket
B. a single object
C. a connected group

6. What does **damage** mean in this book?

*Guardians look out for problems. Space debris is one. It can hit and **damage** satellites.*

A. to fix
B. to harm
C. to eat

Answer key on page 32.

GLOSSARY

civilian

A person who is not part of the military.

debris

Pieces of something that broke or fell apart.

equipment

Tools or machines used to do a job.

hacks

Times when people illegally get information from computer systems.

missile

An object that is shot or launched as a weapon.

orbiting

Following a curved path around an object in space.

satellite

A device that orbits Earth, often to send or collect information.

sensors

Tools that take in information, such as sounds or movement.

TO LEARN MORE

BOOKS

Gagne, Tammy. *Satellites*. Focus Readers, 2023.

Leed, Percy. *The US Space Force in Action*. Lerner Publications, 2023.

Murray, Julie. *US Space Force*. Abdo Publishing, 2022.

ONLINE RESOURCES

Visit **www.apexeditions.com** to find links and resources related to this title.

ABOUT THE AUTHOR

Charles Marlin is an author, editor, and avid cyclist. He lives in rural Iowa.

INDEX

ANSWER KEY:
1. Answers will vary; 2. Answers will vary; 3. A; 4. A; 5. C; 6. B